OWN IT

HOW TO LAUNCH YOUR REAL ESTATE BROKERAGE

ARTHUR DARMANIN

NEIL CRESSWELL

MICHAEL DARMANIN

OWN IT
—How To Launch Your Real Estate Brokerage

Published by Book Ripple Publishing
www.BookRipple.com

ISBN: 978-1-943157-51-8
Printed in the United States of America

To order, go to:
www.Sellstate.com

Foreword

This is about you, a real estate professional achieving your financial dreams.

That is the genuine purpose and focus of this book.

If you are looking for ways to take your income, financial assets, and legacy to the next level … that is what we hope to accomplish together.

Your goals and dreams, if they include having your own brokerage, that is why we are here.

> — Arthur Darmanin,
> Neil Cresswell, &
> Michael Darmanin

Introduction

What is the motivation for becoming a successful agent, becoming a team leader, or even wanting to start a real estate brokerage?

Regardless of your specific goal that motivates you to take action, the desire to advance is a natural progression.

Maybe you are a great agent ... what next?

Maybe you run a great team ... what next?

What is the next step for you? Where do you go from here?

There is a limit to how much you can scale up your business. As an agent, you sell your time. If you are not working, you are not earning.

If you have a team, there is greater income potential. But a team is very time-consuming and expensive. It costs a lot of money to run a team, and you need to constantly recruit and train your team members and generate new leads, among other things.

Is the natural next step to open your own brokerage?

It could be for you. If so, it may be good to know that opening your own brokerage does not mean the end of your selling career. You can still sell. You do need to build the brokerage, which means management is required, but you can still sell if you want to.

Opening your own brokerage also does not mean the end of your team. You can still run your team as you build your brokerage.

For great sales agents and team leaders, you do not have to stop doing what you are passionate about. You can keep that in place while opening your own brokerage.

What is your natural next step?

If you are ready to open your own brokerage, or are considering it in the years to come, then keep reading.

This next step is an amazing one!

Table of Contents

PART 1:

Considering the Opportunity

Are you thinking of opening your own brokerage? Is a brokerage right for you? Does it have the potential for growth that you are wanting? All of these are good questions, and they need good answers.

CHAPTER ONE

Your Next Step

What is your next step to building wealth?

Building wealth through capital investment can be a good avenue for wealth building. If you have the capital to invest, then it might be a great option for you, but few people are able to take advantage of that opportunity.

Perhaps you are in the position to leverage yourself through others and through your real estate experience. If so, then we highly recommend creating a brokerage business to build your wealth.

End Value as a Goal

Let's assume you are making between $200,000 to $500,000 a year through your individual real estate selling or through your team's efforts. You are making good money, but technically your business has no value. You cannot sell the business because you are the business.

On the other hand, a brokerage that nets $200,000 to $500,000 a year can be sold for up to three to five times the net. That is what most accountants will tell you. If you were to sell your brokerage, you would be talking about having $1 – $2.5 million in assets! That is a pretty solid exit strategy, should you ever choose to exit the industry.

How long would it take you to save $1.5 - $2 million?

Want to have your cake and eat it too? You can when you are making $200,000 to $500,000 from your sales and your brokerage is worth $1.5 – $2 million.

For most people, having an asset worth a million dollars is very appealing … but how long would it take to save/acquire an asset worth that much?

For example, if you were to invest in duplexes, deal with tenants, and save every month, it may take 20 or 30 years, or even an entire lifetime, to have an asset worth $1 million. That is a long time to save.

Accumulating assets worth millions of dollars usually takes many years, if not decades, but with a brokerage, that process can be much shorter. In fact, it is possible for brokerages to have a net worth of more than $2 million within a few short years!

And that is real money, real value as a business, that can be bought and sold.

So, what are your plans to create wealth?

Since wealth is created by developing assets and creating assets, there must be some very real plan involved to achieve those goals. If you create a brokerage as an asset, then this applies:

> Whatever the brokerage profits are, 3-5 is the potential multiplier of the asset's value!

Wealth cannot be created by selling your own time.

However, no matter how much you are making from selling or from your team, there is no multiplier. Your asset, in this case yourself or your team, is not something you can sell for more than face value, if you can sell it at all.

The difference between face value (a 1x multiplier) and your brokerage (a 3x to 5x multiplier) is very motivating!

The Power of Duplication

Another important aspect of a true business, as your brokerage would be a business that runs itself without you being involved in day-to-day operations, is that you have the ability to do other things that you want to do.

For example, if you want to sell real estate or build other businesses, you can.

Tip: Most wealth coaches will teach you that to acquire true wealth you need 7 streams of income.

When you have a brokerage in place, you can have a business that runs itself, and that means you are free to create other assets.

Your brokerage is therefore about duplication on many different levels. If you want to create several assets that will have end value, you will have the time to do that. The real estate brokerage business offers you that freedom.

Most people think of a single asset, but with a brokerage, the power of multiplication and duplication really come into play.

Another aspect of creating a brokerage is that it is easier and faster the second time around. Duplication is based on a model, and when you have done it once, you can turn around and do it again with much less effort.

Duplication of yourself and your own selling efforts is technically not possible to do. Duplicating your team and their efforts is a great challenge and seldom possible to do.

But duplicating yourself through a brokerage?

Totally doable!

And when you have done it once, from the recruiting to the building and to the proper team management, it is easier to do it again and again.

Duplication is all about leveraging yourself. With a brokerage, you can do just that.

Taking Decisive Action

It is always time to take action. The best action is the best-planned because it always brings the best results.

How I am going to think differently …

_____
_____
_____
_____
_____
_____
_____
_____
_____
_____

What I am going to do now:

_____
_____
_____
_____
_____
_____
_____
_____
_____
_____

Notes to self:

_____

_____

_____

_____

_____

_____

_____

_____

_____

_____

_____

_____

_____

_____

_____

_____

_____

_____

_____

_____

_____

_____

_____

_____

_____

_____

_____

_____

_____

_____

_____

_____

_____

_____

_____

_____

CHAPTER TWO

The Right Mindset

The right mindset to have before opening a brokerage could best be described as that of an entrepreneur. If you want to build a business, pull all the pieces together and create a company worth millions of dollars ... then you have the right mindset.

What is more, this is also a great opportunity for someone with that mindset.

Is There a Wrong Mindset?

There are some real estate professionals who have said to us:

> "I'm independent. I'm not happy with my current situation and I want to control my own destiny."

This is not the strongest reason or mindset to open a brokerage.

Rather, from experience, we suggest that these independent-minded people find a good company to join, work hard, and go home at the end of the day and not worry about any of the business responsibilities that come with owning a brokerage.

A brokerage is not the best option for controlling people or for those who wish to be alone. In fact, those ingredients will usually cause trouble within any business.

You have to treat the brokerage as a business, a very real business that has risks as well as incredible rewards.

The seriousness of the brokerage business opportunity cannot be treated nonchalantly. We have had some people say:

> "I'm a successful real estate agent and I want to keep a higher percentage of my commissions, so I'll open my own brokerage, get a few agents to sell for me, and it will be great."

It might be great, and hopefully will be, but a brokerage is a business in and of itself and needs to be treated as such.

For others, they explain:

My reasons for opening my own brokerage include:

#1 _____
_____

#2 _____
_____

#3 _____
_____

"I prefer to run my own show and keep everything small and in-house."

This is ideal for many businesses and can work in the real estate business, especially with selling, but a brokerage should be seen as a full-scale business. There should be nothing "small and in-house" about it.

A brokerage has the potential to go big, employ a lot of people, make great money, and sell for millions of dollars. That accurate mindset reflects the nature and potential of the business. To think anything less does a disservice to you.

Your brokerage needs to be seen, thought about, and visualized in large terms.

The Right Mindset to Open a Brokerage

Some reasons are admittedly better than others when it comes to opening a brokerage. Behind every reason is a mindset that accompanies that line of thinking.

We have had successful real estate agents who are making a healthy income and who have some liquidity explain:

> "I want to build a brokerage that allows me to step away from the day-to-day grind."

They want to take time off with their family and be with their children or grandchildren. That is a good reason, and supported with the mindset that they are creating a business now that can run on its own in the future, they are well on their way to their intended success.

Some have said:

> "I want to build for the end value."

Perhaps their goal is to sell the brokerage and step out completely. Maybe they want to invest their profits into other ventures. Either way, they see the opportunity to build true wealth through a brokerage and they are willing to do what it takes to get there.

Others have reasoned,

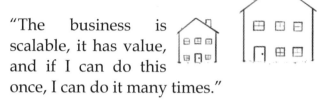

> "The business is scalable, it has value, and if I can do this once, I can do it many times."

For them, building a brokerage and starting another one, then repeating the process, sometimes multiple times over, is their big league goal. They know what it takes to get there, they know the value of creating and replicating a proven system, and they are willing to invest the time and energy to make it a reality.

Even others have explained:

> "I've been selling for years and I want to grow to the next level. I want to help realtors achieve greater success, to build something they can grow and create greater profits from. I want to help others succeed."

There is certainly some pride that comes from that, and those who take this route will not only benefit from a boost to their job description but they will also notice an increase in their own profits.

At the end of the day, there are many reasons to open a brokerage. The best reasons must not only be your reasons, but they also need to have an accompanying mindset that supports that goal.

It's a Numbers Game

In the brokerage business, to make money, you need to close deals. It is a numbers game in that respect. The more agents you recruit, the higher the probability of recruiting good agents. That in turn means more closings, and the more money you will make. It's simple math.

> With sales, possible does not necessarily translate into probable.

The more productive agents are going to generate the most closings. That is always a fact.

As enticing as it might be to envision 10 top agents closing hundreds of deals a month, it is not going to happen. Statistically *possible* does not translate into statistically *probable*, and especially not on a consistent monthly basis.

However, if you have 100 agents, the probability is high that you will reach those numbers and then some. That is why it is a numbers game, and having a brokerage allows you to think and act in bigger terms.

 Part of the numbers game also includes the commissions you pay your agents.

You need to be competitive, but you do not need to give everything away. Having an attractive value proposition that will help the agents close more deals will go a long way in your recruiting good agents.

With real estate brokerages, the possibilities are endless, the options are enviable, and the results are worth every effort.

It is all part of the brokerage mindset.

Taking Decisive Action

It is always time to take action. The best action is the best-planned because it always brings the best results.

How I am going to think differently …

_____

_____

_____

_____

_____

_____

_____

_____

_____

_____

_____

What I am going to do now:

_____

_____

_____

_____

_____

_____

_____

_____

_____

_____

Notes to self:

_____

_____

_____

_____

_____

_____

_____

_____

_____

_____

_____

_____

_____

_____

_____

_____

_____

_____

_____

_____

_____

_____

_____

_____

_____

_____

_____

_____

_____

_____

_____

_____

CHAPTER THREE

What to Expect

Treating a brokerage as a very real business with very real high-profitability potential is a smart and necessary way to look at things. The fact is, treating a brokerage as anything less would be a disservice and undermine your potential for success.

A brokerage is also different from an average business, but in a good way. This is all part of knowing what to expect.

Here are three main differences:

Difference #1 – Low Overhead
With most businesses, overhead expenses increase as the company grows and expands. The greater the gross revenue usually implies a greater and ever-expanding overhead. In fact,

overhead typically grows in direct correlation to revenue.

It is a chase, and at the end of the day, hopefully the business owners have done everything right and are earning more than they are spending.

What are the real costs of opening a brokerage?

Unlike your typical business, in the brokerage business, your overhead does not change very much. Your gross income continues to increase and grow ... while your overhead remains fixed.

Yes, you read that correctly! Your gross income goes up and up, yet your overhead remains relatively the same. That means the profit margin can be as big as you want it to be. Those are encouraging numbers to everyone in business!

Some agents considering a brokerage have asked:

> "But won't my overhead increase at a certain point?"

Yes, at a certain point the overhead does increase, but it is further down the road than most realize. This is because the only time your overhead will increase, assuming you are running a proper

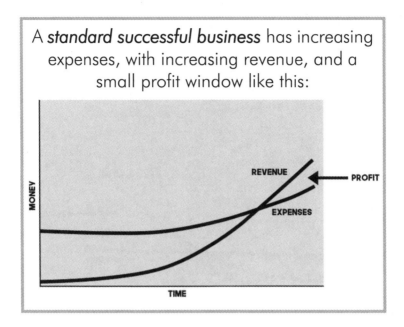

A *standard successful business* has increasing expenses, with increasing revenue, and a small profit window like this:

business model, is when you have well in excess of 50 agents working in your brokerage!

And even then, the overhead increases minimally as a result of adding more support staff to your company. That is why a brokerage is such a phenomenal business!

When you look at the brokerage business as compared to any other business, think about the fact that the agents working for you do not require you to pay them wages, nor do you need to pay them benefits.

You do not even have to provide them with leads like you do when you are running a team.

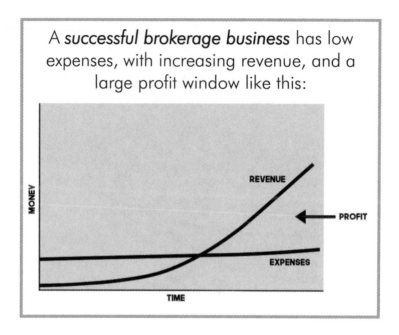

A *successful brokerage business* has low expenses, with increasing revenue, and a large profit window like this:

With a team, they are on a commission split, such as a 50-50 or 60-40 split, because you have to give them leads. Without your leads, they are not going to stick around.

Not many business models exist that can put a large number of people to work for you (some of them seven days a week, 60 hours a week) and build considerable wealth and value for you without the need to pay them a salary or benefits.

Compare that to other businesses and see if you find one that compares!

Difference #2 – No Inventory Cost

When it comes to inventory, a brokerage is uniquely suited. There is literally billions of dollars in inventory, and the best part is, it costs the brokerage nothing!

This unlimited inventory of homes for sale in the MLS system comes at no cost to you.

You can advertise the inventory, sell this inventory, or keep the inventory in stock. What is more, the inventory is continually changing and adjusting to the market. It is fresh and updated as more and more houses are added to the MLS.

> The MLS inventory and its millions of dollars in commissions are available to you ... at no cost.

What's more, unlike other businesses, if the price of the inventory is reduced, there is no cost absorption by the broker. At worst, the total commission to the office may be slightly reduced unless your agents are on a flat transaction fee, in which case there is no cost to the broker at all.

What other industry offers a better inventory situation?

As a broker/owner, you do not even have to personally go look at that inventory.

The agents do that for you, and yet you get a piece of the action from everybody in the office.

We often say:

> "When you really think about it, this is a fantastic business model! There is always a risk with every business, but this is a far lesser risk than a lot of businesses."

The fact that the inventory comes at no cost to you plays a huge part in keeping expenses low. That gives you ample room to grow, provide competitive commissions, and generate good profits.

There are very few business models that can offer what a real estate brokerage does.

Difference #3 – Low Capital Required

One of the first questions we are often asked by interested parties is:

> "What is it going to cost me to open a brokerage?"

The fact of the matter is the amount of capital required is not great. But this is not to diminish real costs either. You do need some capital to set up your office and carry it for the months it takes to start generating sufficient income, but you would need that with any business.

However, start-up capital does not need to include inventory or supplies. Not having to pay for inventory or supplies usually associated with a business launch is an immediate huge savings for you, the broker.

Low Risk, High Reward

A brokerage is without question a fantastic business model, but we will never kid you … no business venture is a walk in the park. If it were easy, everyone would do it.

Every business launch is going to take work. A brokerage has many advantages that make it a truly incredible opportunity, but it will take hard work and effort.

It's a brokerage … think differently.

This is the only business model we know of that allows you to capture all the upside (low overhead, no inventory costs, and low capital required) of a high-potential business without having to shoulder a lot of risk.

In addition, within two to three years, it is completely feasible that your brokerage could be highly profitable … and worth 3 to 5 times the net profit should you want to sell it.

That looks something like this:

- Business making good yearly profits
- Business worth 3-5x profits
- Business growth all within 2-3 years

What other business venture can realistically make that claim and back it up?

That is why we are continually explaining to people:

> "It is critical, if you are thinking of going into the brokerage business, that you see this as the opportunity it really is."

A brokerage is a phenomenal business, so treat it as such. Do not let anything slow you down. Build it right, build it big, and there is no reason why the profits back to you should not exceed your expectations!

Taking Decisive Action

It is always time to take action. The best action is the best-planned because it always brings the best results.

How I am going to think differently …

_____

_____

_____

_____

_____

_____

_____

_____

_____

What I am going to do now:

_____

_____

_____

_____

_____

_____

_____

_____

_____

Notes to self:

_____

_____

_____

_____

_____

_____

_____

_____

_____

_____

_____

_____

_____

_____

_____

_____

_____

_____

_____

_____

_____

_____

_____

_____

_____

_____

_____

_____

PART 2:

Taking Action

You have decided to open your own brokerage. It is time. The opportunity fits well with your current position and plans. The next steps require action, all with the intention of creating the ideal brokerage, one with the greatest potential for success.

There are many questions that you will be asking yourself as you move down this journey. One of the most important questions will be if you are better off to do this on your own or with the help of an existing franchise system.

Deciding on whether or not to align yourself with a franchise is a big decision and one that should be considered in your business plan. Even if you decide to go the independent route, it would behoove you to take some time and research the various real estate franchises if for no other reason than to learn about what they offer and what tools and ideas you should offer yourself.

All franchises are not created equal. As you speak with them you should ask yourself if you would join the company as an agent. If not, then understand why not. If so, then understand why you would.

From a broker's perspective, you must also understand what tools and support the franchise will provide you. How is the franchise going to help you recruit agents? What tools do they offer? What training and support is there for you and your future agents? Are you able to replicate these systems and tools on your own?

Costs are also a vital part of the equation. What costs and fees are associated with joining the franchise? Are these costs fair? Are these costs explained or lumped together under a general royalty?

Once you have established answers to those questions, then you must consider the business model as a whole. Does the franchise system make financial sense? There are some models whose platform is to offer 100% commission to the agents and make the fees lower than all competitors in the area. While this may attract a lot of agents, you need to question the caliber of these agents and if there is enough money coming into the office to sustain it.

Other franchises use their strong brand as the primary driver with the belief that agents will join simply based on the name and reputation. Does this make sense? Do they have offices in your area? How are those offices performing?

Finally, some franchises strive to provide the best value proposition to brokers and agents. Does their value proposition offer something new or exciting to the market?

As with the original set of questions, you should always ask yourself if these are tools and systems that you can provide on your own. If you can, then your next consideration is the cost of doing it on your own. Just because you can doesn't necessitate that you should. Is it possible but too expensive to provide yourself? What is the timeframe to setup all these systems and implement all these tools? What is the opportunity cost while you get all of these things implemented and in place?

As you will come to learn when you open a brokerage ... you are in competition with everyone else (big or small, franchise or independent) whether you like it or not! The fact of the matter is, if agents join your office, they did not join someone else's, and vice versa.

Be properly prepared going into this decision. The rest of this book will help guide you through your preparation.

CHAPTER FOUR

Traps to Avoid

Learning from our mistakes makes us wiser, but when you are stepping into something new, especially a business venture such as opening your own brokerage, would it not be helpful to know what to expect?

But common mistakes, by their very nature, are often traps that can be avoided.

Over the years, many new brokers have asked the same questions in one way or another:

> "What are the most common mistakes, traps, or roadblocks of brokers … and how can I make sure I don't do the same thing?"

Great question!

Here are our combined answers:

Trap #1 – Lack of a Business Plan

We have found the most common out-of-the-gates error is that of trying to start a brokerage without a true business plan.

Relax. You do not need to spend months creating a massive business plan, but you do need to do your homework so that you are truly ready to launch your brokerage.

By "true business plan" we mean a plan that:

#1 – Lists your true estimated expenses:

> With just a little bit of research, you can find out what rents are going for, what the commission structure should be, how many agents you feel you need to hire, and the estimated time for all of this to happen.

#2 – Includes your magic profit-breaking number:

> How many agents will you need, based on the average number of closings you feel is

YEAR 1: P&L Statement - Estimates	
Agents Hired	tracked per month
Total Agents	tracked per month
Transactions Closed	tracked per month
Note Avg Fees on Comm	

a conservative estimate per agent, to get each month to turn a profit?

#3 – Details the amount of money you will invest into the venture:

You need to look at your personal finances and calculate just how much money you have to invest in this venture. Do you know what your living expenses are now, including all the variables such as rent, mortgage, utilities, taxes, etc.? How many addition costs are you expecting to add with your brokerage? Do you have enough money for both personal and business?

#4 – Outlines your ongoing plans within the business:

If you continue to sell real estate, that is fine, but how much time are you going to devote to recruiting? Your recruiting efforts will reflect the growth of the office.

YEAR 1: P&L Statement – Estimates	
INCOME	
Commission Income	tracked per month
Advertising Income	tracked per month
MSA Income	tracked per month
E&O Insurance	tracked per month

If you keep selling, then you should consider a recruiter. You cannot do both jobs well. The same applies to being the manager. If you are going to hire help, how do those factors, expenses, timetables, and commissions work out in your plan?

When you do your homework, the answers to these important questions will become evident.

YEAR 1: P&L Statement – Estimates	
EXPENSES (1 of 2)	
MARKETING	
Newspapers/Magazines	tracked per month
Signs	tracked per month
Brochures	tracked per month
Logo	tracked per month
Technology	tracked per month
Printing	tracked per month
Classified Ads	tracked per month
Website	tracked per month
Lead Generation	tracked per month
ADMINISTRATION SERVICES	
Accounting Services	tracked per month
Manager Wages	tracked per month
Admin Wages	tracked per month
Lead Generation	tracked per month
Manager Bonus	tracked per month
MEALS & ENTERTAINMENT	
Conference	tracked per month
Hotels	tracked per month
Meals	tracked per month
Travel-Airfare	tracked per month

At that point, you will be ready and prepared to take the next step, whatever that may be.

How quickly you come up with a plan directly affects the speed in which everything gets off the ground. Consistent daily action on your plan is the answer. The speed part is up to you.

Working on your business plan gives you the knowledge you need. You will understand the cost, the true cost, and that is vitally important.

For example, if you are currently earning

YEAR 1: P&L Statement – Estimates EXPENSES (2 of 2)	
OFFICE EXPENSES	
Copier Lease	tracked per month
Copier Maintenance	tracked per month
File Storage (app files)	tracked per month
Insurance: E&O	tracked per month
Insurance: Liability	tracked per month
MLS/Board Fees	tracked per month
New Company Reg Fees	tracked per month
Bank Fees	tracked per month
Postage	tracked per month
Rent	tracked per month
Supplies: Kitchen	tracked per month
Supplies: Office	tracked per month
Utilities: Cable/Internet	tracked per month
Utilities: Electric	tracked per month
Utilities: Cell Phone	tracked per month
Utilities: Water/Sewer	tracked per month

$100,000 a year from your personal production and you want to start a brokerage, is it accurate to assume the $100,000 will continue? The same applies if it is $250,000. From our experience, personal production goes down in the first year because opening a brokerage takes time and effort. What then will your actual income from personal production be? You will have to make a conservative estimation based on your research and careful planning.

Yes, it may take some time to work out all the details, but you can do it.

Trap #2 – Bad Office Location

The second most common error is the location of the office. Quite often, brokers do not do a proper demographic study to find out where prospective agents actually live.

Why is this important? Because as a brokerage, you are looking to serve the agents, not the prospective home buyers or sellers.

YEAR 1: P&L Statement - Estimates INCOME	
NET INCOME *Before Taxes*	*tracked per month*
Capital Expenditures	*tracked per month*

Here is the fact of the matter:

> Just because agents will drive 20 miles to show a property does not mean they want to drive 20 miles to the office.

That means one thing:

> Agents like their office to be close to where they live.

That makes your job, and your brokerage location, a simple matter of finding out where the agents live.

It is tempting to put the office close to where you live. Naturally, you don't want to drive too far to work either, but that proves the point! Think of your future agents. Make it convenient for them, for in so doing, you are making it beneficial for you!

Map it out. Find out where your competition has their offices. Where are they located and why are they there?

Suppose you find five brokerages on one street. You may be thinking:

> "I don't want to be there. That is where all the competition is."

Stop for a moment. Your primary customers are agents. You not only want to attract them, you want to make the location convenient. Being near other brokerages will not hurt you.

Ever wonder why restaurants are usually located near each other? The reasons include convenience and proximity to customers. The same applies to your search for a location.

Maybe you were thinking:

> "To avoid the competition, I should locate the office a few streets away."

The location must be a good one, supposing the five offices that are already there are doing well, then the agents must not mind the commuting distance. So an office a few streets over may not actually help you at all.

Your location needs to be ideal for your agents.

In fact, the quickest way to do your demographic study is to find out where all the agents are ... and that is where you want your offices!

Starting in the wrong location will make the trip to success much more difficult than it needs to be.

Make it easy on yourself and decide to open your brokerage near where your clients are.

Trap #3 – Thinking Too Small

The third most common mistake when opening a brokerage is thinking too small. It sounds odd to say, considering the magnitude of the decision and the opportunity of opening a brokerage, but small thinking can cripple a brokerage from the start.

The thinking usually goes like this:

> "I'm going to start small and only rent a little executive center or a 500-square foot office, and as I make money I will scale up."

It does not work that way. It cannot work that way.

Ask yourself honestly why an agent who works for a successful firm with a nice office in a nice building with nice facilities and in a great location would leave all of that to come work in your little executive center.

Would you join your own brokerage?

It is admittedly a hard sale. The grow-as-you-go is always true in some respects, but when it comes to an office building and location, you must have something attractive to be attractive.

For others, the small thinking is from a different perspective. Their mindset is one that says:

> "I've done well in my business, so I'm going to open my own brokerage to save money."

Opening a business to save money is not really a business at all. It is a personal savings program at its best. This mindset is really a defeatist attitude and the result of this small thinking is going to be a small business that does not grow.

If you are going to open up a business, go big! You open a business to make a profit and to create something that has end value, so why not go all out? That is what you really want for your brokerage.

Avoid the Traps

The way to avoid these traps is summed up in three words:

Implement Your Plan.

If you plan in advance, you will have a business plan that gives you the necessary information to launch your business on solid answers, solid facts, and solid estimates. Trap #1 avoided!

If you plan in advance, you will know your demographics and choose a location that is ideal for your clients. Trap #2 avoided.

If you plan in advance, you will open up as a proper business in a good location with sufficient square footage, the proper amount of furniture, and adequate administration staff. This leads directly to a business that can be profitable and that can create a lot of end value. Trap #3 is avoided.

All this planning in advance leads to one huge piece of your brokerage success. It is the answer to perhaps one of the biggest challenges that brokerages face. It is this:

> Are you sufficiently funded?

Opening a brokerage is not a bootstrap-to-success type of business to launch. You know that from all the preparation you have put into the venture. And when you have taken the time to do the homework, have

If you are afraid of the competition, don't open a brokerage business. Competition is proof that the brokerage business is profitable, otherwise no one would be doing it. If you do it right, you will get more than your fair share!

pressed in and answered the necessary questions, your planning will pay off.

That is because:

> You are able to get the funding you need only when you know how much funding you actually need.

We have found that after you have avoided these three traps, most often you will have the capital you need to open your brokerage.

You are well on your way to a successful brokerage!

Taking Decisive Action

It is always time to take action. The best action is the best-planned because it always brings the best results.

How I am going to think differently ...

_____
_____
_____
_____
_____
_____
_____
_____
_____
_____

What I am going to do now:

_____
_____
_____
_____
_____
_____
_____
_____
_____
_____

Notes to self:

_____

_____

_____

_____

_____

_____

_____

_____

_____

_____

_____

_____

_____

_____

_____

_____

_____

_____

_____

_____

_____

_____

_____

_____

_____

_____

_____

_____

CHAPTER FIVE

A Well-Planned Entrance

They say we have only a few seconds to make a first impression. As much as we may like or hate that reality, it is still a fact.

Similarly, a well-planned entrance as a brokerage will do wonders for your first impression to the agents you need to attract.

The best way to make a good impression is to be prepared. Though perfection is not required, being as prepared as you can be through due diligence is a must.

Answering these questions will help.

Initial Questions to Answer

As we already discussed, the ideal location for your brokerage is where the majority of the agents are already working.

There are several other specific details about the building that need to be part of your equation.

Those specifics include:

Square footage:

> Q: Is there a sweet spot for square footage to start with?

> A: The sweet spot is somewhere between 1,500 to 3,000 square feet.

Expected occupancy:

> Q: How many people are you planning to have at that location?

> A: Size wise, you need to be ready to accommodate the number of agents you plan to recruit.

Location:

> Q: What are you looking for when you scout locations?

> A: Never forget that your office needs to be around the competitors.

Secondary Questions to Answer

Armed with what you now know about your location, there are other details that you must be aware of before you commit. For example:

Floor level:

> Q: Is the office you are considering on the 2nd floor or higher?
>
> A: There is nothing wrong with the second floor, or higher, but there needs to be an elevator for elderly or handicapped people. This is important. Without access to your office, you are excluding some of your clients. You must also realize that being on the 2nd floor will make walk-in business nearly nonexistent.

Do your homework. Find out where the agents work and why.

Parking:

> Q: What is the parking like?
>
> A: There needs to be ample room for around 10-15 cars, counting agents and their clients, to be there at any given time.

Typically, you will only have 5-10% of your agent population in the office at any given time.

Access:

Q: Is easy access for agents to swing by the office essential?

A: Agents like to be able to pull in and out with easy access. They will need to drop in, pick things up, drop things off, meet a client, and more. Access needs to be easy and open.

Signage:

Q: Do you have a sign and exposure for your offices and agents?

A: Signage is a good option to have, and it increases your branding and leverage. However, if it costs you an extra $10 a foot, then you may want to go without it. Use other means to increase your awareness that is not so costly.

Visual appeal:

Q: What does the building look like? Is it a nice building or is it run down and old?

A: The building itself is a strong indication of what is inside. Without question, the building needs to look nice and have good curb appeal.

Safety:

Q: Is it safe? Can agents safely walk to their cars at all hours of the day?

A: When the sun goes down and your agents feel unsafe, that is the kiss of death to your brokerage. Realtors must feel safe and comfortable. Since they will drop by on weekends to handle details, it must be safe. If safety is a concern, whatever the time of day, look for another building.

How can you help your agents maximize their ROI?

Best Foot Forward

How you answer these questions means everything to how others, especially the agents you are trying to attract, perceive you.

Put your best foot forward by answering these questions well. You will be glad you did, and so will your agents when they come join you!

Taking Decisive Action

It is always time to take action. The best action is the best-planned because it always brings the best results.

How I am going to think differently …

_____

_____

_____

_____

_____

_____

_____

_____

_____

_____

_____

What I am going to do now:

_____

_____

_____

_____

_____

_____

_____

_____

_____

_____

_____

Notes to self:

_____

_____

_____

_____

_____

_____

_____

_____

_____

_____

_____

_____

_____

_____

_____

_____

_____

_____

_____

_____

_____

_____

_____

_____

_____

_____

_____

_____

CHAPTER SIX

Buy, Lease, and Build Out

You need the right building for your brokerage. That is the bottom line. But whether you buy it, lease it, or build it out is entirely up to you.

In your decision making about your building, keep this one detail in mind:

Make sure it is a win for you.

It is not a requirement that you buy and own your office space as a broker. You certainly do not have to … but if you can, if you have the resources, and everything about the building and location is a good match, then feel free to.

There is nothing wrong with buying the building that houses your brokerage.

Before you make that big purchase, however, make sure you have answered all of the tough questions. Only then should you consider it.

Prerequisites to Buying

If you are leaning toward buying the building or simply considering the option, here are 4 recommendations to keep in mind:

#1 – Do not buy a building in a rundown area:

> Regardless of whether it is a great deal or not, your agents—statistically more than 50% of agents are women—will not feel safe working out of an office in a questionable area. That is a business-killer decision right out of the gates.

#2 – Make sure you have adequate funding:

> For many new brokers, funding is a challenge. Do you have enough working capital to purchase the building and carry the costs of running your new brokerages? If so, then that opens up more options, but if not, do not spend the time looking to buy. Focus instead on leasing and getting your business up and running.

#3 – Do not be fooled by a good deal:

A deal is only good if it is really and truly good for your brokerage. If you have the money and resources to buy the building, be careful that you are not suckered in by a seemingly great deal that doesn't meet the proper brokerage requirements.

#4 – Be flexible and smart:

Now, supposing it really is a good deal on the building and you have the money to buy it … but it is not a good location for your brokerage. Do not buy it for your brokerage, that is plain enough, but if you want to buy it and lease it out to somebody else, go for it. Then find another building to lease for your brokerage.

Prerequisites to Leasing

In most cases of new brokers, leasing a building or unit is the best option. This is for the primary reason of freeing up your time and capital for the highest and best use … growing your brokerage.

Another reason that leasing is usually the best option is that it gives you more flexibility on many levels, and that is helpful when you are in the head-down and focused mode of launching your business.

> Never compromise your business by buying or renting in a bad location.

Quite often, after three to five years of growing the business and creating good cash flow, the brokers find a building (or land) in the right location and buy (or build).

When cash is flowing in, buying makes great sense.

In the meantime, if you are leasing, here are 3 recommendations to keep in mind:

#1 – Require the landlord to fix up/build out the building before you move in:

Most often, landlords are more than willing to promise to revamp a building that you are looking to lease. The question you must ask is, "When will you do it?" We have seen it take a year or two for landlords to do the work they promised. The best way to avoid this hassle is to require the landlord to complete the work beforehand. At the very least, a good portion of the work needs to be done and all remaining work needs to have specific dates attached, including deep savings for you if key dates are missed. Your business needs a nice building when you start, not years down the road.

#2 – Ask commercial real estate agents about current and soon-to-be-available office space:

Leasing an office is not the same as buying a house. Many times commercial agents know of tenants who might be moving out in the next 30 or 60 days. They know of space before it is put on the market.

#3 – If nothing is available in your ideal location, do not be discouraged:

If it is a good spot for your brokerage, it will probably be busy. However, there is always a way. Start with commercial agents as they have a very good pulse on the businesses in your desired area. Call on several agents. Get all their minds going on your behalf.

The Build Out

More times than not, the office building you choose to lease or buy will need to likely build out your location to accommodate your plans for the number of agents you plan to recruit.

You do not need an architect at this point. What you need is an expert in the business who can help you design the few thousand square feet office area into an area that can fit your growing number of agents.

> You need a balance of office space, conference rooms, and open business space. The key word is "balance."

It needs to be nice and look good to work for the personnel, but above all, it needs to be efficient.

Keep in mind that you are going to need some client rooms and conference rooms. Those are a must.

You are also going to need some office space because some of the top producers or teams will want to have office space within your space. In case you are wondering:

> You cannot turn a few thousand square foot office building into sufficient office space for 50-100+ people to have personal offices, if your plans called for that many recruits.

 It cannot be done, but rest assured, it does not need to be done.

You need to build out your building, whether you bought it or you leased it, so that you have some very specific key elements, which are the following:

- **Office rental space:** Some office spaces that you can rent to those who need the space within your building.

- **Multi-person space:** Some multi-person office space for agents or teams who at times need a private area to work in.

- **General business area:** A business area that agents can use when they are in and out of the office, allowing them to print contracts or fliers, do research online, make calls, and do whatever they need to do.

- **Conference rooms:** Conference rooms where agents can meet and sign contracts with home buyers. You need at least one (two being better, depending of course on your number of recruits) of these rooms, each holding a maximum of 4-8 people.

Agents increasingly work from home, but they still need to have an office to work from if needed. Most importantly, however, they need a nice office building to bring clients to for the initial meeting to the final "make the sale" moment. Providing the office, conference room, décor, accessibility, comfort, and safety for that transaction is reason for the entire building.

We have found that most agents will work out of the open business area, so this needs to be an important part of your build out efforts.

Before you buy or lease, remember the build out costs. Look at the building. If it is a hollow and empty "vanilla box," the cost to make it what you need is going to be more than a building that already has most of what you want.

Keep this in mind as you proceed.

…

So whether you buy or lease, before the necessary build outs, it is entirely up to you. It is your decision. But always make sure the building is a win for you and a win for your brokerage.

When you and your brokerage win, so does everyone else!

Taking Decisive Action

It is always time to take action. The best action is the best-planned because it always brings the best results.

How I am going to think differently …

_____

_____

_____

_____

_____

_____

_____

_____

_____

_____

_____

_____

What I am going to do now:

_____

_____

_____

_____

_____

_____

_____

_____

_____

_____

_____

_____

Notes to self:

_____

_____

_____

_____

_____

_____

_____

_____

_____

_____

_____

_____

_____

_____

_____

_____

_____

_____

_____

_____

_____

_____

_____

_____

_____

_____

_____

_____

PART 3:

Attracting the Right People

Growing your brokerage is the goal. Making it as big as you envisioned is the plan. That is going to require a mixture of the right ingredients.

In order to have a chance of reaching those goals, it is vital that you implement the correct internal team in order to cover every key position.

To begin with, depending on the number of agents you want to recruit, it may require a fulltime recruiter. Recruiting cannot be a hit or miss affair. Someone doing fulltime recruiting is a must.

An office administrator will also be required. The administrator position has evolved over the years from a receptionist who simply answers the phones to someone who requires computer skills and is able to assist with office technology, CRM management, email campaigns, and much more.

The reality is that agents direct their calls to their smartphones and transactions are managed through paperless software platforms, which eliminates the need of the old-fashioned receptionist. He or she must have a good understanding of computers and the ability to learn how to use today's technology. This individual will be an intricate part of the recruiting, onboarding, and training process for people who join your office.

Once your team is assembled, you will have the right pieces in the right places, which is the ideal scenario for your growth.

CHAPTER SEVEN

10 Proven Ways to Attract Agents

As a brokerage, you need agents. Even the most well-known brokers and brokerages across the nation need agents. Without agents, there are no sales, and the business ceases to exist.

Agents are the lifeblood of the business. You, as the broker, also provide them with tools that make their lives a whole lot easier.

Or at least you should. Without a compelling reason to change, agents will stay right where they are.

To get agents to join your brokerage, you will need to be prepared. This is what preparation to attract agents looks like:

Attraction #1 – No Waiting Required

Agents do not like to wait, especially in matters that have to do with you, the broker. To attract agents, you must have the necessary amenities right then and there.

The general-use business office, for example, needs to be built out and ready to go before they come to work for you. If you ask them to wait for any necessities, you will not be well received.

> Always remember: Bootstrapping can work to build a team, but it does not work as well when building a brokerage.

Those who are willing to wait are those who have invested in your company, and if the agents are not investors, you cannot ask them to wait. That is a risk they are not willing to take.

When there is no waiting, you have the attention of the agents.

Attraction #2 – Offering Something Better

When you offer better than what agents currently have, be it the building, location, amenities, sales split, environment, culture, training, technology tools, you name it, agents are interested.

 Never ask agents to give up what they already have if you do not offer better.

76

That is an immediate red flag. They naturally think, "Why would I give up what I already have?"

Sometimes offering equal, as compared to better, is attractive, especially if there are other benefits that outweigh what they are giving up. Having said that, if all you offer is equal to what they have now, you cannot expect them to go through the process of moving to receive the same benefits they already have.

How you present your offer to prospective agents will also have a great impact on them making a decision to join you. Using visual aids such as PowerPoint presentations, videos, live demos, etc. is a must in today's world, especially if you are making the claim that you are technologically advanced.

Lastly, preparation is everything. Be organized. Make sure your presentation is complete. Shuffling papers and looking for stuff while presenting will diminish your professionalism.

Attraction #3 – A Realistic Perspective

Agents want to know that you have a realistic perspective. They want to know you see things how they really are and are not starry eyed and living in a dream world.

For example, we have found great salespeople and great team leaders who honestly believe people will join their brokerage simply to be near them. They believe they are so incredible that agents will make sacrifices just to be with such awesome talent.

The cold, hard truth is that a great personality is not enough. It is certainly good to have, and people like working with truly great people, but personality does not pay the bills.

They say love is blind in a relationship, and as true as that might be, it is not the case in business.

Agents will join your brokerage when you offer more of what they want, which is more than what they currently have. They need to believe that they will close more deals by working with you. Your personality is a bonus, not sufficient bait.

When you know, as agents already know, that you have a realistic perspective of yourself and the facts of the business, they will find that very comforting.

Attraction #4 – Proof You Have What It Takes

Agents want to know you have what it takes. They are watching. They are talking. They are also hoping you win, but they are not willing to take a risk with you (after all, they are not investors), but they are interested.

This goes both ways. Be careful that you do not jump into being a broker simply because of what other people may have said. Agents will often say, "Oh, if you're going to open up, I will come with you."

What they mean to say is, "If you have what it takes, I'd be very interested in working with you." That is a big IF. And there is no time frame attached to their statement.

Basically, you must recognize that agents have a wait-and-see attitude. They are going to wait and see, and you cannot rush them. They are probably thinking:

- What's your office going to be like?
- Where is your office going to be located?
- Are my commissions safe with you?

They have a lot of questions they want to see answered, but all the while they will tell you, right to your face, "Absolutely, I'm going to come over when you open. Yeah, for sure!"

You cannot bank on it, so do not open your brokerage based on their promises. Even if 10-15 agents tell you the same thing, you must always remember:

Agents will come over when you prove you have what it takes.

Attraction #5 – Be Boldly Competitive

Competition is serious business. Agents want to know that you are serious about your brokerage succeeding.

We have seen brokers naively think that if they do not aggressively compete with other brokers, even the bigger brands, then they are not in fact in competition with all the other brokers.

> Always ask yourself: "Why would agents leave where they are and come work for me?"

That is not the case at all, and agents know that! The very moment you open your brokerage and try to convince an agent to leave wherever they are to work with you, you are in competition. And that is very serious business.

Increasingly, real estate brokers are very competitive. All the other brokers are after those same agents, not just you. Everyone is competing.

Agents know that, so just embrace that fact and

call it what it is. Then make sure your offer is better than your competition!

Attraction #6 – A Seamless Transition

Switching from another brokerage to yours is quite a process. It always is, but if you can make that transition a seamless process, you will get far more agents as a result.

The transition process includes such menial yet necessary things as new business cards, signs, websites, and email addresses, not to mention notifying all their clients. They may even have listings that they may or may not be able to bring over.

> Agents are there to sell. That is their #1 job. That is always the target.

It is not an easy thing, but the easier you can make it for them, the happier they will be. In addition to all that you offer, you make it easier by taking care of these basics (business cards, signs, emails, etc.) with them.

That goes a long way in making the transition process a seamless one.

Attraction #7 – Starting the Right Way

Having a proper office and sufficient office space, including an office administration, is very attractive to agents. It gives them confidence in you and the opportunity you are offering them.

We have found that the brokers who want to bootstrap their business by starting with just 500 square feet for an office, with or without furniture, and no administrative help, inevitably have a very hard time attracting agents.

It is simple:

Starting too small is a big turn off!

Agents cannot help but think that bootstrapping means there is no funding and the budget is tight, which means they may not get paid depending on cash flow. That negative thinking, brought on by the start-small-and-grow-as-you-go mentality they see in the office, is a clear sign to run away!

Starting the right way does not mean starting huge and going into massive senseless spending, but starting with a "big" mindset is very attractive to prospective agents.

The day you open the doors, your office needs to look and feel the same way as if you had the number of agents you want to recruit already working there. That is what starting the right way looks like, and agents love it!

Attraction #8 – No Risk

Agents take enough risks as it is. They do not want to take any more. As the broker, when you do all you can to shield your agents from risks, they will appreciate it. That in turn frees them up to do what they are good at ... getting more sales.

The risk of the brokerage is yours. You may be great at selling, but if you have to sell to pay the bills, you are putting unnecessary risk back on to your agents. They don't want it!

Agents want you to know and operate by this fundamental truth:

> "What got you here won't get you there."

Being great at selling or building a team might have gotten you here, but it will not get you there. Your agents want you to succeed, as that success directly affects them as well, so you cannot necessarily rely on what worked in the past to build an incredible future.

Agents want you to know that, for in so doing, you are shouldering the risk. That is much more attractive than passing it on to them.

Attraction #9 – Curb Appeal

An attractive office is a must. We have seen brokerages that were disgusting. They literally were dumps. Those agents who worked there would probably have joined another brokerage in 10 seconds if the opportunity presented itself.

Agents want a nice and professional place to meet their clients. They want to be proud of the building, inside and out. This brings stability, confidence, and respect, all of which works in your favor with your agents and their clients.

> Top-producing agents do not want to meet their clients in a co-working space or a coffee shop.

All of this creates the right environment. Then the agents, whether they are selling a $2 million house or a $150,000 condo, are proud to bring in their clients.

Attraction #10 – Getting a Fair Trade

Agents are going to bring you a book of business, their own hard-worked-for business, and they want a fair trade in return.

 They know what's in it for you. What are you going to give them in return?

What you offer is your value proposition, and it had better be good. When what you give them in return is equal to or more than they expected, you will be exactly what they are looking for ... and that is very attractive!

It is a proven fact that agents want these two things above all:

#1 — to close more deals

#2 — save more time

Those are two of the strongest motivators for agents. Without offering that, they are not interested ... but if you can provide that, they are incredibly interested in working at your brokerage!

...

When all is said and done, people resist change. That is a fact of life that affects everyone, in every industry, all the time.

You cannot be perfect and you cannot make everyone happy, but everything you do to make your brokerage attractive is going to help agents get over their personal resistance to change.

Since change is painful, every effort you take to ease the pain means more agents coming your way!

Always remember that you are asking agents to give up what they already have to join you. Put yourself in their shoes. Make your value proposition a good one. When your offer would move you to take action, then you know you are on target.

Attracting agents to your brokerage is as easy as that!

Taking Decisive Action

It is always time to take action. The best action is the best-planned because it always brings the best results.

How I am going to think differently ...

_____
_____
_____
_____
_____
_____
_____
_____
_____
_____
_____

What I am going to do now:

_____
_____
_____
_____
_____
_____
_____
_____
_____
_____
_____

Notes to self:

_____

_____

_____

_____

_____

_____

_____

_____

_____

_____

_____

_____

_____

_____

_____

_____

_____

_____

_____

_____

_____

_____

_____

_____

_____

_____

_____

_____

CHAPTER EIGHT

Your Future Agents Really Care About Your Location

As a broker, your clients are agents. Location matters to them more than it does to you! Always keep that in mind.

The home buyers and home sellers are important, of course, but their locations are fixed. You cannot do anything about where the houses are located, so everyone willingly works around that factor in the sales equation.

What is never a willing workaround is the brokerage office in a bad location. Agents will refuse to join your company, regardless of what you offer, if your location does not work for them.

The best location advice for where to open your brokerage is always the same:

Find the place where most realtors are, and that is where you want to set up shop.

It is hard to go wrong when that is the foundation for your brokerage.

Where Agents Actually Live

It may sound a bit odd to say this, but agents do not live where you want them to live. They live wherever they have chosen to live.

Developing areas:

> Agents do not live in new developing areas. There may be 100s or 1000s of homes going up on a side of town, but odds are, agents do not live there.

Future developing areas:

> Agents do not live in areas that are about to be developed. An area about to be developed has nobody living there, and that means the agents do not live there either.

High-end markets:

> Most agents do not live in ideal high-end markets. Yes, it is nice to sell homes in those areas, but the majority of agents do not live there.

Putting an office in developing areas, future developing areas, or high-end markets is, sad to say, a foolhardy move. Don't do it, no matter how tempting it might be.

What Is a Good Location Worth?

Can you handle an extra $1,000 or $2,000 per month for a better location?

It is something to think about. Most often, in looking for location, you will have several good or even great locations scouted out for your brokerage. One of those places is probably a bit more "ideal" in its location … and it probably costs more per month.

> When it comes to attracting agents, remove as many objections as you can.

Is it worth it? Sometimes it pays to look at it this way:

If this location helps you add a few more agents, it will more than make up for the extra expense.

The tough decision is really a no-brainer when you look at it like that.

> Prosperity does not come by cutting and cutting. Rather, prosperity comes from increased revenue.

In time, you will find that the rent (or your mortgage payment, if you purchased the building) is not your main concern.

Why not? Because you will eventually come to understand that your energy must always be focused on increasing revenue and not on decreasing expenses.

That may not be a no-brainer just yet, but in time you will see that to be the case. Yes, keep an eye on your expenses, but what brings in more revenue must always be the focus.

We have found that it is possible to save your way to bankruptcy. Conversely, a revenue stream that is steadily increasing is not headed toward bankruptcy at all.

...

At the end of the day, your job as broker is to attract agents. That is the big picture, the only picture, and you must keep that front and center in all your location decisions.

> Everything revolves around the one thing … attracting agents.

That is the name of the game for you. Without agents, you have nothing, but with agents, you have unlimited potential. Yes, it is a tough business, but it is a great business with an incredible business model.

And it's yours if you want it!

Taking Decisive Action

It is always time to take action. The best action is the best-planned because it always brings the best results.

How I am going to think differently …

_____

_____

_____

_____

_____

_____

_____

_____

_____

_____

What I am going to do now:

_____

_____

_____

_____

_____

_____

_____

_____

_____

_____

Notes to self:

_____

_____

_____

_____

_____

_____

_____

_____

_____

_____

_____

_____

_____

_____

_____

_____

_____

_____

_____

_____

_____

_____

_____

_____

_____

_____

_____

_____

_____

_____

_____

CHAPTER NINE

How to Recruit Successfully

Recruiting is probably the number one reason that you will succeed as a broker. It is that important.

To reach your potential, to achieve the success you want for you and your brokerage, it comes down to your recruiting.

Every broker must learn, accept, and live by these two basics of recruiting:

> **#1 – Recruiting takes time.** You have to spend your time recruiting. Make your schedule around your recruiting.

> **#2 – Recruiting is not just going to happen.** You must plan for it and follow up on that plan. Recruiting only happens on purpose.

As a broker, it is vitally important that you understand what it takes to recruit. Yes, it will take some time to learn all the ins and outs, but it is important that you begin with the expectation of becoming a master at recruiting.

Literally, you must master recruiting. To reach your full potential as a broker, you absolutely must become a master of recruiting.

Become a Master Recruiter

A master recruiter understands that recruiting is a full-time job, depending on the number of agents you want to recruit. When you open your brokerage, a tremendous amount of time needs to be spent on recruiting. Regardless of how much time you spend at the office, you will need to make recruiting part of your entire day.

Your first waking thought every morning needs to be about recruiting and your last thought at night needs to be about recruiting.

Food and water, oxygen and recruiting, that is how high recruiting needs to be on the priority list as you launch your broker's business.

As you recruit to your brokerage, your agents prospect to get more clients and more sales. Recruiting and prospecting are equally as important. Agents who prospect will make more sales, just as brokers who recruit will have more agents.

Time and time again, we have seen this fact come into play:

> Brokers who become master recruiters are the ones who are most likely to succeed.

Make it your aim to become a master recruiter.

If you are considering a franchise, one of your primary questions should be aimed at what the franchise will do to help you with recruiting. Naturally you do not expect them to do it for you, nor should you believe any franchise that tells you recruits will automatically join you due to the brand, reputation, or anything else they are offering. However, you do need to see what tools and guidance they offer in the way of recruiting.

Usually the difference between a brokerage that succeeds or fails boils down to one thing: recruiting.

It is also important to realize that attempting to attract quality agents simply by "giving the farm away" and paying out 100% commission and having fees lower than the local competitors is a race to the bottom and not a viable and sustainable business model.

What matters is how the franchise is going to enhance your value proposition. How will they help you help agents close more deals?

Recruiting needs to be part of their culture as it must be part of yours.

Massive Action Required

What it really takes to succeed at recruiting is massive action. Usually, that means picking up the phone every single day and calling agents.

If the goal is to build a large office quickly, then scheduling 10 appointments each week is what it will take. That means you will need to call 50-60 agents to fill your weekly time slots.

Of those 10 appointments, a few will cancel, leaving you with 5-6 interviews. And out of that, you hope to sign 1-2 to your brokerage.

Do you know what it means as far as:

- Getting the contact information
- Number of calls per day
- Amount of time to call
- Recalling if needed
- What you will say during the call
- How you will follow up
  - What if they say "yes"?
  - What if they say "no"?

- How you will handle them saying they are happy where they are?

It takes a lot of action to sign up 1-2 agents a week, and that means a lot of processes in order to handle all the details surrounding that action.

Yes, it can be complicated. You have to be more diligent and more purposeful and intentional with recruiting than agents need to be with prospecting. It is a much more complex sale.

> The better the agents, the longer it will take to recruit them!

Regardless of the size of the office you want to build, the goal must be broken down into the number of agents you need to recruit on a monthly or even weekly basis.

Most brokers need to look at recruiting as a skill they need to acquire by practicing it over and over. Truly, recruiting is habit forming.

Build Your Pipeline

Recruiting is not just about making a presentation. It involves asking the right questions. Everyone has a motivation or a hot button, and it takes effort to find out what motivates your prospects.

By asking the right questions you will be able to understand where they are coming from and what they are really saying. A "no" could mean a variety of things, such as:

- "Not right now."
- "You haven't convinced me."
- "Not a chance, ever!"

Regardless of what the prospective agents say, you need to put those agents into your recruiting pipeline. If they said "yes," what are your next steps?

What if they said "no"? Those leads are not simply thrown out. The worst thing you can do, and we have learned this from experience as well as from working with countless brokers, is to fail to follow up with those who give you a "no."

Instead, every "no" agent goes into your follow-up pipeline. This process is physically impossible to do manually, so you will need a software program that helps you divide your leads into at least three piles, typically As, Bs, and Cs.

What that looks like is this:

- The agent who says, "I'm busy, call me in two months," goes into your pipeline.

- The agent who needs more information goes into your pipeline.

- The agents who said they would join you when you opened your brokerage go into your pipeline.

- The agent who fails to show up at your appointment goes into your follow-up pipeline.

Here is a secret:

> Absolutely everyone goes into your follow-up pipeline.

Keep your pipeline full of prospects. The more it overflows with leads the better.

Recognize also that building your pipeline is a process. It takes some time, and you will win some and lose some, but the more you use it, the more you stock it, the greater your rewards will be.

It is a combination of phone calls, interviews, and follow-ups. It is a process that has a beginning but no end. Getting in the habit of filling your pipeline is the best habit you can create for growing your brokerage, and the faster you do so the better!

Forming the Recruiting Habit

These tips will help you form the necessary habit of recruiting:

Tip #1 – Expect to spend the time:

> Why don't more brokers grow? Because they don't recruit.
>
> Why don't they recruit? Because they don't have time.
>
> Why don't they have time? Because they are manually doing all sorts of things, such as paperwork and managing of the business.
>
> You must not only expect to spend time recruiting, you must actually spend the time recruiting.

Tip #2 – Hire a recruiter:

> Recruiting efforts must reflect the number of agents you want to recruit. That means you basically have two choices:
>
> A) Hire a manager so you can recruit.
>
> OR

B) Hire a recruiter so you can manage, sell, or whatever you planned to do.

In case you wondered, it is fine to not be the recruiter yourself. If you do not want to do it, that is okay ... but do not lie to yourself and say, "I'm going to do it," when you know full well you are not going to do it.

Regardless of what your growth goals are, someone has to do the recruiting. If you cannot do it, hire someone who can help you, whether that person takes over the management tasks, recruiting, or both.

> If you are bootstrapping your brokerage, you will never have enough time to recruit.

Whatever suits you best, do that. But keep in mind ... if nobody is recruiting, your office will not grow!

Tip #3 – It takes more time than you think:

Most brokers working 50 hours a week think they will be able to spend half their time recruiting.

105

We have found that part-time recruiting generates very few sign ups. In fact, in many cases, the actual number of recruits from part-time recruiters was almost zero.

It takes time to effectively recruit, and usually it takes more time than you think.

Tip #4 – Cold calling experience pays off:

Being great at selling is helpful when it comes to recruiting, especially if you have no fear of cold calling. The ability to cold call is extremely beneficial when it comes to recruiting.

However, many great salespeople assume they will automatically be incredible at recruiting. Hopefully they are, but home buyers and sellers (the clients of agents) are vastly different from agents (the clients of brokers).

If you are not afraid to pick up the phone and call people, that is definitely a plus. But if you have a phobia of using the phone or fear rejection, open the brokerage but hire a really good recruiter.

The Role of Technology in Recruiting

Technology is a wonderful tool, but recruiting is much more personal, manual, and hands on than sending emails, texting, and scouring the internet. Here is the fact:

> Email is great, but like all technology, it is not the complete answer to recruiting. It is not even close to being the best answer.

The most productive agents will not be enticed to join your brokerage because of an email. They require physical touch and verbal face-to-face communication.

It is important to remember:

- **Technology has not replaced the telephone.** Mobile phones allow you to make calls from wherever you are.

- **Technology allows you to look up agents and look at their productivity.** You know who your clients are. Now you can check them out before you even meet with them.

- **Technology enables you to track agents and see what they are good at** (do they list a lot, do they sell a lot, what is the usual price range, etc.) **so you can tell what they might be wanting.** For example, if you know an agent is selling a lot and has a bad commission split, you know he or she is potentially looking for better returns on their efforts.

- **Technology reveals what a brokerage offers their agents.** If they provide few tools, have a minimal business center, or have a negative working environment, you know exactly what their top agents might be interested in gaining.

Recruit Strategically

Some brokers recruit randomly, basically trying to recruit every agent who moves. Not all agents are created equal!

You need to look at recruiting a little differently. Do that by dividing the agent population into three segments:

A) The top 20%
B) The middle 60%
C) The bottom 20%

Based on this breakdown, you then approach each agent grouping with a separate game plan.

The Top 20%

The top 20% are of course the top producers who bring in the vast majority of the sales. There are not that many of them, so you keep them on your to-get-on-the-team list and constantly look to recruit them. It will probably take you more time and effort, but top producers are very few and far between, so stay on them until you get them.

The Middle 60%

The middle 60% are the medium agents who produce a fair number of sales. Collectively they sell enough to boost your yearly sales to what it needs to be. If you have enough of these middle 60% agents, you can hit your goals for your brokerage.

Technology has not replaced the telephone!

The Bottom 20%

The bottom 20% … you do not want them. As you find them, keep their names in your system. Check up on ones you hear about, on the chance they have moved up to the middle 60%, but for the most part the bottom 20% will do more harm than good to your brokerage.

In a nutshell, this is your market of agents. It is up to you how you will stock your brokerage. This is where the numbers are, where the money is, and where the rubber meets the road.

You have to be careful how you recruit because your yearly sales are a direct reflection of your recruiting efforts.

The beauty of it is the fact that your potential, your incredible future as a broker, is right there in the palm of your hand. Your recruiting efforts can bring you rewards that are 10x, 20x, and even 50x the effort you put into the process now.

Recruit strategically and it will pay off amazingly over time!

Taking Decisive Action

It is always time to take action. The best action is the best-planned because it always brings the best results.

How I am going to think differently ...

_____
_____
_____
_____
_____
_____
_____
_____
_____
_____

What I am going to do now:

_____
_____
_____
_____
_____
_____
_____
_____
_____
_____

Notes to self:

_____

_____

_____

_____

_____

_____

_____

_____

_____

_____

_____

_____

_____

_____

_____

_____

_____

_____

_____

_____

_____

_____

_____

_____

_____

_____

_____

_____

_____

CHAPTER TEN

CHAPTER TEN

How to Recruit Top Producers

Top producers will be a profitable boost to your brokerage. You want them, but it is important for you to know that you can survive, even thrive, without them.

Building your brokerage business goes on with or without the top producers. Thinking, "I have to have 10 top producers or we will never make it," is not the truth. It is a position of weakness.

Instead, look at it this way:

> Build your brokerage bigger and recruit as many top producers as you can along the way.

Your company can produce hundreds of sales every year with only the middle 60% of agents. Of course, having top producers on the team makes the process faster and easier, but it is important to know it is possible nonetheless.

As for the top producers, the top 20%, they are a unique brand of agent. The more you know about them, the more likely you are to recruit them.

Here are several secrets about top producers that will be helpful as you grow your brokerage:

Top Producers ... Change Slowly

We have found on average that it takes two weeks to recruit a typical agent away from one brokerage to another.

How long does it take to recruit a top producer?

One day? One call? One introduction?

Probably much more than that! It could take several weeks to several months to recruit big leaders to your brokerage. It may even take a year, but it will be worth it in the end.

Constantly keep reaching out to top producers because they make decisions more slowly than other agents. They have their reasons, so you need to stick with it.

Top Producers ... May Not Be Happy

Do not assume top producers are happy where they are. You never know, if you catch them at the right time, at the right moment in their career, they can be moved.

It is a big mistake to assume the top producers are happy where they are. You never know until you ask.

Top Producers ... Want to Make More Money $

Quite often, top producers are working for a brokerage that offers a commission split that is not as favorable to the top producer as it could be.

By no means do you give away the farm to recruit top producers. In your research on top producers and the brokerages they work for, odds are that the agents would make more money if they worked at your brokerage.

> All top producers want one thing: more time.

Making a lot of sales does not necessarily mean making a lot of money. Keep that in mind as you recruit top producers. Most top producers want to increase their income level.

Even if the top producers are on a favorable commission split, this does not mean they are satisfied with how much money they are making. In some cases, top producers are looking to increase their sales volume but are so bogged down handling the details of their current deals that they cannot see how it is possible to make more money by closing more deals.

Top Producers ... Want More Time

Some top producers may even tell you, "I don't want to close more deals."

What they are saying is that they do not have enough time in the day to handle any more business.

That is a shame! The obvious answer would be to help the top performing agents have more time to do what they do best, and that is make more sales.

All top producers want more time. If you can provide that for them, they will be very inclined to join you.

Top Producers ... Need Assistance

 Based on the fact that top producers want more time, a creative way to address that need is to provide them with assistance and guidance.

What top producers want to hear is a broker who says, "You are doing great, but you are killing yourself. You need a buyer's agent or two. Let me help you do that."

Getting involved and helping them rather than simply assuming they need nothing from you will do wonders in attracting top producers to your brokerage.

How much of the money coming into your brokerage is staying?

Top Producers ... Hate Drama

Top producers get things done. That is how they maintain their high level of productivity.

One key to their success is their efficiency. If anything messes with their system, their ability to do the deal, their well-oiled machine is out of whack. Efficiency grinds to a halt.

Who is frustrated the most? Who puts out the fires? Who cleans up the mess? Clearly, it is the person who cares the most. The less-productive agents and over-worked brokers may not even lend a hand.

Frustrated top producers are ripe and ready to join your brokerage if you can provide them with a drama-free environment. That is incredibly attractive.

Top Producers ... Hate Being Ignored

Head down and working hard is a recipe for progress, sales, and hitting records. It is, oddly enough, often a way to get ignored.

The squeaky wheel gets the oil, and if top producers are quietly getting the job done, it is probable that they are also being ignored.

What they want is not that hard to provide:

- In meetings, saying a simple "good job" or "thank you for always doing a great job" will go a long way in making top producers feel acknowledged and appreciated.

- Brokers often have leads coming in that they hand off to less-productive agents because they think the top producers already have enough business. That hurts the top producers' feelings more than it does their pocketbook.

 • Top producers are ambitious people, so helping them understand the business where they currently are or how to get to the next level will show them that you care.

Top producers hate being ignored. If brokers are ignoring them, and you recognize this error and have a remedy to fix it, your brokerage will be a whole lot more attractive.

Top Producers ... Like to Be Heard

Believe it or not, top producers are willing to get less per sale in the commission split if you are meeting a need that is more important than money. But how would you know that ... if you did not ask them?

It typically takes 3 meetings and 3-6 months to recruit top producing agents.

Everyone has different wants, needs, and desires. Top producers are no different. What is more, things change. What was motivating a few years ago may not be as powerful as it once was.

Maybe top producers are interested in more tools, less drama, more time, more appreciation, greater investing opportunities, more time with their family, and much more.

119

When you ask, "What is it that you want to be or do?" and then really listen for the answer, you may be surprised by what you hear.

For example, a top producer might say, "I'm making $650,000 a year, but I miss my family." Your goal is clear: help the agent reach or exceed that mark AND be able to spend more time with his or her family.

Seldom do people ask top producers what they really want. Sit down and find out where they are and see if you can help them accomplish their dreams. If so, you will have yourself a top producer!

Do Not Be Intimidated by Top Producers

Most brokers are intimidated by top producers. They are thinking things like:

- "How could I possibly recruit that agent?"
- "I'm okay at selling, but she is a sales machine!"
- "My best year was 25 sales and he has hundreds each year!"
- "That agent sold $20 million last year and I sold only $2 million!"

However the logic goes, the results are the same

... brokers are afraid to call on the top producers. But you know better.

Take the position as that of a coach. No coach is as good as the athlete, but the coach helps the athlete perform even better. It is not a comparison or competition between coach and athlete or broker and agent.

> What is their hot button? Your job is to find out what the agents really want.

Rather, it is a team with a focus on maximizing success. Every athlete and every top producer wants that, and so does every coach and broker. You must accept this truth and then live by it as a broker:

> Who cares that the agent is better than you ... that is the way it is supposed to be!

As a broker, you are the coach. Your job is to look at things from different angles, to look for ways to boost sales, and to look for ways to make the top producers even better.

Throw aside the intimidation. Instead, look for ways to coach that person to a greater level of success, and your mindset will change.

Then pick up the phone and set up an appointment!

Setting Up the Appointment

The most effective way to reach out to top agents is to call them. Do not rely on email or text or other forms of social media.

Be bold and pick up the phone. That is your best chance for setting up the appointment.

You do not have to get super creative with your marketing brochures, advertising campaigns, or direct mail pieces. The top producers are not going to look at those at all. They are looking for a phone call, so pick up the phone!

Yes, you do need to have the systems in place, a strong value proposition, and a building that is ready to handle top producers. You need to be set up to capitalize on them joining your brokerage, but as soon as you are ready, reach out to them.

It might be hard work to build a brokerage and recruit amazing people, but it is not rocket science. You can do this!

During the Appointment

When you do talk with prospective agents, be they the top (20%) or middle (60%), your job is to find out what they want. This is especially true of the top producers.

Your value proposition is important, but not as important as the agents' wants and needs. So ask them a lot of questions.

Usually, in an interview with a brokerage, you will hear all about how great they are and all the reasons why you should work for them.

Instead, your job as the broker is to find out what their hot buttons are, what is their pain, why would they want to move to your brokerage?

When you find out what moves them, what they want, what they are keenly interested in, you have built a level of trust and rapport that goes a long way in creating a lasting relationship.

Nobody wants to work for someone who is non-caring or someone who would deceive you with recruiting gimmicks. That is especially true of top producers! Treat every agent at every appointment with respect and honesty. In doing so, you will demonstrate true leadership, which is attractive to everyone … especially top producers!

When you do this, top producers will want to work with you. And that is the way it should be.

Taking Decisive Action

It is always time to take action. The best action is the best-planned because it always brings the best results.

How I am going to think differently ...

_____

_____

_____

_____

_____

_____

_____

_____

_____

_____

What I am going to do now:

_____

_____

_____

_____

_____

_____

_____

_____

_____

_____

Notes to self:

_____

_____

_____

_____

_____

_____

_____

_____

_____

_____

_____

_____

_____

_____

_____

_____

_____

_____

_____

_____

_____

_____

_____

_____

_____

_____

_____

_____

CHAPTER ELEVEN

Create a Recruiting and Prospecting Culture

The recruiting part of the equation is yours to master, as you are the broker. But as you live and breathe recruiting, it will foster a healthy prospecting culture as well.

Your agents need to be focused on prospecting as much you are on recruiting, and they are more likely to do so when they see you leading the way.

A recruiting and prospecting culture is the ideal environment for everyone in your offices to max out their potential. Over the years, we have seen this to be true:

> The most profitable brokerages are the ones that have a recruiting and prospecting culture.

That is always the case.

Culture Begins With Recruiting

A recruiting and prospecting culture begins with a strong focus on recruiting. What does that look like on a practical basis? The answer is full-time recruiting.

If you want to build a large brokerage, you will need to be recruiting full-time or have someone in your brokerage who is recruiting full-time. That means you should net anywhere from 7 to 10 agents a month. In a year, that translates to somewhere between 85 to 120 agents.

What that means to your bottom line is another matter entirely!

We suggest that you pay your recruiters a base salary along with a bonus based on performance. What that amount is depends on your average sale price and everything else, but compensation should be a combination of base salary and performance efforts. The biggest money, the biggest potential for income, should be in the performance part of the equation.

What this exactly looks like in dollar amounts varies from area to area, so you will have to determine what the salary and performance bonuses are. The recruiter does, however, need the ability to earn six figures.

 If you have managers who also do recruiting and generate 5-10 agents a month, they need a similar base salary plus performance bonuses. You will probably not pay a manager/recruiter as much as a full-time recruiter, but results should always be the determining factor. Allow people freedom to excel, and pay them accordingly.

Help your recruiter by holding him or her accountable. Have a weekly meeting to discuss the interviews, who is in the pipeline, who would be likely to join and when, etc. At minimum you should be having this meeting and offering support and guidance as necessary.

You can further assist your recruiter by using technology to put together a list of agents for your recruiter to target. The quality of agent that you would like to target is up to you. What are your minimum standards? Is it 6 closings a year, 8, or more?

All agents want big potential income ... so make it possible!

Recruiters are like everyone else. They enjoy success. As a result, they often have a tendency to go after the "low hanging fruit," which means new agents. This happens because those agents are often easier to recruit. While recruiting new agents is perfectly fine, new agents require a tremendous amount of time and effort to get them properly trained and prepared. They also come without an existing book of business. Be sure to identify who you would like to target and make it clear to the recruiter so there is no confusion in the process.

A culture built on recruiting leads naturally to an increase in prospecting.

Training to Prospect

The goal is always to get more sales, and adding more agents to your brokerage is going to do just that.

From the agents' perspective, getting more sales begins with more buyers and sellers added to their client lists.

As the broker, you are the coach. You are creating a culture that is alive and growing. To accomplish this, you need to position your efforts and training and money according to this one goal:

Help everyone be more and do more.

That creates a very strong culture of recruiting and prospecting.

It is one thing to say you want to "help everyone be more and do more," but it is another matter entirely to actually do it! Make sure you do, for it has tremendous dividends.

The best way to help your agents be more and do more is through training. The more skillful they are, the better results they will get and the more satisfaction they will have from a job well done.

Rejection has a way of wearing you down to the point of no longer taking action. All forward motion ceases and agents quit or cease to make any more sales.

If you can help agents overcome rejection, that is money directly into everyone's pockets!

As you lead the way with continual recruiting, you are demonstrating to your agents how to overcome objections and to keep moving forward.

That is the ideal role model, but further training of your agents is needed. You can:

- Encourage them to hit their goals.
- Help them with proven scripts.
- Offer training sessions to the team.
- Tell them what to expect.
- Show them how to overcome objections.
- Bring in top producers to demonstrate.
- Motivate them to take action.
- Teach how to follow up.
- Cycle the entire staff through trainings.

- Repeat the training often.
- Offer bonus trainings for getting ahead.
- Show them how to use technology to close more deals.
- Guide them on how to optimize their CRM instead of just telling them they need one.
- Provide technology tools and make sure you have the accompanying training sessions and workshops to properly educate your agents on how to use the tools to avoid frustration. Never assume because you offer a tool that the agent will use it. Be sure to get them up to speed.

The best way to break through the wall of rejection is by training and by taking action. More often than not:

The best trained team always wins.

When your brokerage is properly trained, you can expect to hit your 100, 200, 500, or even 1,000 or more sales per year. Whatever your goal is, you will be incredibly happy, and so will your agents.

Your Role as Broker

As broker, if your goal is to build a "mega office," you should aim for 2 recruits joining your brokerage a week. What that translates into is you setting up about 10-12

New agents who have just completed their training course are looking for a job. Believe it or not, brokers seldom call them.

About 50% will receive a marketing piece in the mail, but few will actually get a call. There are 100s of agents coming into the industry every single month.

Be the first to call them!

appointments each week. From those 10-12, we have found that 4-5 will not show up for one reason or another.

When it averages out, your goal for 2 recruits each week requires full-time recruiting and a lot of hustle, but it is doable. It has been tested. It works, and we have done it.

With proper training, recruiting scripts that are proven to be effective, and sufficient follow up, you can do it. You and/or your full-time recruiter can bring in the agents you need to make your brokerage what you intended it to be.

Your value proposition is ultimately the deciding factor for your prospective agents. If you know what they want — because you asked questions and listened for their answers — and you can meet that very real need, then your value proposition is going to be very enticing.

When you bring all these details to the table, there is no reason why you cannot hit your marks.

Remember, everything you do as a broker to help your agents close more deals is also going to help you recruit more agents. That is the culture you want to foster.

It looks like this:

Step #1: Help your agents close more deals

Step #2: You recruit more agents

Step #3: More agents perform well

Step #4: Everyone makes more money

And that is what a culture of recruiting and prospecting is all about!

Taking Decisive Action

It is always time to take action. The best action is the best-planned because it always brings the best results.

How I am going to think differently …

_____

_____

_____

_____

_____

_____

_____

_____

_____

_____

_____

What I am going to do now:

_____

_____

_____

_____

_____

_____

_____

_____

_____

_____

_____

Notes to self:

_____

_____

_____

_____

_____

_____

_____

_____

_____

_____

_____

_____

_____

_____

_____

_____

_____

_____

_____

_____

_____

_____

_____

_____

_____

_____

_____

PART 4:

Building a Successful Brokerage

When it comes to opening your own brokerage, you want everything to be lined up and in order. The responsibility for success rests on your shoulders, but having to create all the tools or learn via trial and error are not a responsibility you need to carry. We believe that when you do the necessary research into your options, be it going solo or aligning yourself with an existing franchise model with existing tools and expertise, that the results should always be better.

CHAPTER TWELVE

An Eye for Profitability

Becoming a broker and creating a profitable brokerage is going to take time and effort on your part.

You are going to become a great leader in the process as you train, coach, and build up the many agents who work with you.

The requirements placed on you, which are all centered around meeting the needs of those in your brokerage, are completely missed by most brokers. They assume they already know everything needed to be a successful broker.

Here is a truth to ponder:

> If you already knew everything, you would already be doing it.

You can be an incredible broker, and an incredibly profitable broker at that, but it will require you to know how to meet the needs of everyone on your team. And THAT is admittedly a very tall order!

Be What Your Brokerage Needs

From recruiting to retention, to training, to the culture building, to training new agents, training mediocre agents, training top producers. There's so much you have to know, and you literally cannot hire a coach to do all that.

> If you want to hire a recruiting trainer, do your homework. Make sure there have been proven results.

You must be the coach.

Now, you will find a lot of trainers who will offer (for a lot of money) to train you on how to recruit. Some of these recruiter trainers are good, others are bad, but recruiting is only one part of the overall training you need to best service your agents.

Finding a coach who teaches how to recruit is one thing, but you will not find a coach who teaches you how to train your team. That is a big job, one that is yours to carry.

There are no coaches who teach you how to coach. If they know how to train on a subject, they will offer their skills for a price, do the training and leave, but nobody is going to teach you how to train. They don't do that.

That means you must develop the skills. You must learn yourself how to do what it is your team needs to learn. This includes such things as training, support, systems, and technology.

It is a lot to learn, but somebody has to do it. Of course, in time you can train someone else to do a specific training.

Here is another truth that will help you be an even better broker:

> There are no shortcuts.

Being a top agent or being great at closing or being amazing at converting are good skills, but that is not going to meet all the training needs within your brokerage.

We have seen new brokers take the I'll-figure-it-out-along-the-way approach to building their brokerage. That is the same as saying:

> "I'm okay with taking 10 years or more to slowly, by trial and error, figure this out."

Are you really okay with that? Don't be.

Going slow has many hidden costs, such as carrying all the office expenses for year, not to mention the loss of potential profits, loss of end value, and loss of quality agents. This is not to mention the opportunity cost of moving and developing slowly.

All combined, we have about 100 years of combined experience in this business. We would challenge you with this:

> If you are going to be a broker, be a great broker and max out your business opportunity!

The more you understand what you are getting into, the more likely you are to build a successful brokerage business.

Stay on Track
You may see a broker with 120 agents and assume that person has it all figured out. Dig a little deeper and you may find:

- The brokerage is doing 5-10 deals a month … combined!

- The broker is out selling to pay the bills.

- The agents are deadbeats with high commissions yet no drive to do anything more than sit in the office.

> What you don't know is bad enough; it's what you don't know that you don't know that has the power to really hurt your brokerage.

That is not a brokerage you want to own.

You want a business that is thriving, alive, and full of passionate agents who are pushing to excel.

You build the business right, you hire good people, and you train them well … and you will get good results!

That is a business you can be proud of.

Taking Decisive Action

It is always time to take action. The best action is the best-planned because it always brings the best results.

How I am going to think differently …

_____

_____

_____

_____

_____

_____

_____

_____

_____

_____

What I am going to do now:

_____

_____

_____

_____

_____

_____

_____

_____

_____

_____

_____

Notes to self:

_____

_____

_____

_____

_____

_____

_____

_____

_____

_____

_____

_____

_____

_____

_____

_____

_____

_____

_____

_____

_____

_____

_____

_____

_____

_____

_____

_____

_____

_____

CHAPTER THIRTEEN

What It Means to Train Your Team

Most brokers think that training is just a weekly motivational sales meeting. That is not training.

Brokers then wonder:

- Does a sales meeting here or there count as training?

- Does having a title company or mortgage company come in and give a speech (along with a box of donuts) count as training?

- Does a "lunch and learn" meeting count as training?

- Does sitting around telling stories count as training?

None of this is bad, and though some of the content might actually be very helpful, it does not count as training.

What Training Really Is

One way to look at training in a brokerage is to think of it this way:

> If you were brand new, yet had a burning desire to succeed as an agent, what would you need to know to succeed?

Then you intentionally do everything you can as the coach to answer that question. From the little facts to the big picture, you put it all on the table. Those agents who are hungry to learn and excel will do just that.

With that in mind ...

Training Is Structured

> Training must to be structured, have set time frames, and cover specific subjects. Newer agents have an extraordinarily high failure rate simply because they are not properly trained and prepared. The real estate industry has a bad habit of being a loosey-goosey industry and as a result, sales meetings tend to follow no established order, which leaves success to random chance. Agents, especially new ones, need structure if they hope to stick around long enough to become highly successful agents.

Training Starts at the Beginning

Everyone needs to learn how to be a good agent. You start at the bottom, with the basics, and you work your way up. This includes learning how to prospect, how to get leads, how to do a proper open house, how to talk to "For Sale by Owner" prospects, and much more. Knowing what to say and how to say it is vital to their success as agents, and it starts at the bottom and works its way up.

> As a broker, training is the best way to help your agents to the next level.

Training Brings Greater Results

Agents who close 3-4 deals a year could easily close 6-8 deals. The same holds true for agents who close 20-30 deals a year or even those who close 50-60 deals a year. There is always room for improvement and getting greater results. If you give them proper training, you will witness that new reality coming to pass.

Training Is Scheduled

Agents need a calendar showing when the training sessions are and what the subject matter is. Busy agents do not want to show up to a training they have already taken several times. They do not need to be there. Conversely, allowing agents to see what is coming up and when will allow them to build attendance into their busy schedules. Schedule all the trainings.

Training Is in Levels

You need to think of training as having three levels: for the newbies, for the middle 60%, and for the top producers. For the newbies, offer training in a structured 4-8 week courses, and make sure you hit all the levels repeatedly. For everyone else, be sure to schedule at least a month in advance. Keep everyone updated so they know what the training covers and when it is taking place.

Training Needs a Curriculum

In college, you buy a book. There is substance, there is the beginning, and there is the end. You need something similar. Once that is completed, once they have gone through all the training and have practiced all the parts, more advanced training is then made available. With a clearly defined curriculum, the training is progressive. That benefits the agents at all levels. The more professional the training, the better agents will feel about attending it.

Training Involves Scripts

A true coach will say, "Yes, you need to call on prospects, but this is how you do it." They are going to tell you what to do and then show you how to actually do it. With calls, that involves scripts. Resistance to scripts is common. People say, "I don't like scripts. They feel like canned presentations." Until you are getting better results than the person who uses scripts, it is best to learn scripts. Once you own a script and you know it well, it becomes more natural and comfortable for you.

Training Includes Many Parts

Agents need to know how to handle every part in the process, from setting a business plan to looking at houses, to setting up a sphere of influence, to building their CRM, to implementing their technology to building their website, from preparing buyers to negotiating contracts, and much more. Every part is important. Good training will train on every single piece of the puzzle.

Training Requires Accountability

Training includes accountability. They have assignments and homework, then they return several days later and tell how it went. Learning from experience is a great teacher in this industry, and specific assignments that are discussed as a class do just that.

Training Specifics for Top Producers

Top agents gain very little from the normal sales meeting. They need far more than a non-focused, general information meeting. Offer specific trainings, such as: the best place to spend your money for lead generation, the latest marketing tools, or how to build a team. Provide the content they want and need, and make sure it is posted well in advance. Ideally, do this at least once a quarter with just your top producers.

Training from Top Producers

Remember that top agents need to be appreciated, listened to, and valued. They may have joined your brokerage because they were neglected. Do the opposite. Give them room to shine. Let them share their insights or tips for the other agents who are learning. Don't go to the extreme and turn the top producers into trainers, but definitely tap into their expertise. That will make them feel appreciated, praised, and needed, while at the same time not taking too much of their time.

> Training tip: Ask top producers what their needs are, and then meet those needs!

Training Is for Better ROI

At the end of the day, the goal of training is to bring greater results, both for your business as well as for the individual agents who are learning, improving, and excelling.

- The newbies advance into the middle 60% where they begin to hold their own and make sufficient numbers of sales.

- The middle 60% boost up their numbers to the point that they may even double their sales and income. Some will even move up into the top 20%.

- The top producers never want to leave for another brokerage because you are serious about developing and coaching to the next level. That is, by the way, the ultimate insurance that your top agents never leave!

Training shows your agents that you have a genuine interest in helping them succeed. Everyone wants that! They are making a lot of money, and so are you, but you are doing your part for them.

That is an incredibly strong value proposition, one that no agent will want to leave.

Taking Decisive Action

It is always time to take action. The best action is the best-planned because it always brings the best results.

How I am going to think differently ...

_____

_____

_____

_____

_____

_____

_____

_____

_____

_____

What I am going to do now:

_____

_____

_____

_____

_____

_____

_____

_____

_____

_____

Notes to self:

_____

_____

_____

_____

_____

_____

_____

_____

_____

_____

_____

_____

_____

_____

_____

_____

_____

_____

_____

_____

_____

_____

_____

_____

_____

_____

_____

_____

_____

_____

CHAPTER FOURTEEN

How to Make the Offer Completely Irresistible

You are ready to open your brokerage and you are committed to being the best broker and best coach agents have ever known.

Well done!

The next step is to make your offer so irresistible that within 12-24 months you have 30, 50, or 100 agents working with you (whatever your goal is), cranking out the sales in a culture that is full of recruiting and prospecting.

All of this is doable.

At this point, you are probably thinking, "Okay, so what exactly do I do now?"

What Do You Do Now?

Many people will strike out and launch their own brokerage independently. There are thousands of independent brokers out there, but they are for the most part all very small.

Being independent can work, but we have found that it makes the going all that much tougher. It takes extra time, effort, and money to try to figure everything out for yourself. If you do that, progress is slow and that can be discouraging.

Is the ROI really an ROI for you?

We would not suggest taking the independent route if you want to grow a profitable brokerage as quickly as possible.

There is so much to do, learn, and implement when it comes to recruiting, marketing, advertising, prospecting, retention, and business growth. Having help in these areas is vital to your growth. You are on your own if you are independent.

For that very reason, many brokers decide to join a franchise. You could do that as well, but make sure you read and understand all the fine print before you jump. For example:

- What is the commission structure?
- What are the hidden fees?
- Who pays those hidden fees?

- Does the training have a cost?
- How often are the trainings?
- How are they going to get you started?
- Will agents join you when they learn what the fees really are?
- How will they actually help you open your doors?
- What technology tools do they offer?
- How much does the technology cost the agents?
- How are they going to help with recruiting and training agents?
- How will they help you build the right culture in your brokerage?
- Will their systems make my life easier or more difficult?
- How is back office paperwork treated?
- Are people reachable when help is needed?

> Make the offer irresistible by offering agents exactly what they want and need.

Always remember that in the compensation plan, you never get something for nothing. If the franchise company is offering a huge sponsorship program, what is their split?

Always remember:

They give nothing away for free, so find out how the deal works for everyone involved.

As a broker, you need to know what the franchise offers you as well as what the franchise offers your agents. That is because:

If anything inhibits your ability to recruit, it is also inhibiting your ability to make money.

What is your ROI for joining a franchise? There must be a win in the equation for you. For example:

- Will they save you years of work?
- Will they save you thousands of dollars?
- Will they help make sure you are in a really good location?
- Will their training help your agents reach their maximum potential?
- Will their technology help you and your agents?
- Will they be able to guide you through the process of building a brokerage?

There is another option. We believe it is even better than operating independently or joining a franchise. Our suggestion is that you consider becoming a broker with Sellstate.

When You Join Sellstate

When you become a broker with Sellstate, we immediately put a lot of things on the table for you:

Sellstate Provides Broker Training

We continuously mentioned the challenges of trying to open your own brokerage. Even if you are able to avoid most of the pitfalls that commonly hamper new brokers, you still find yourself in the impossible situation of trying to build out an office, hire administration staff and possibly a recruiter, set up all the technology, and implement a proper training schedule, all while trying to keep your sanity.

Sellstate prides itself on having a tremendous startup program for both new brokers and independent brokers looking to expand their operations. We truly cover the "A-Z" on getting your brokerage up and running.

Before you even get your doors open, Sellstate will be transforming you into a master recruiter. The scripts, techniques, and audiovisual aids are all at your disposal from the very first day.

As with agents, the training never stops! We communicate well with our brokers, and that includes conference calls, meetings, and conferences, all with the intent of making you better, more efficient, and more effective.

With Sellstate, you will not have to worry about looking elsewhere for guidance as you go from starting a brokerage to growing one to the highest level.

Sellstate Provides Agent Training

Prospective agents are looking at you and thinking, "How is joining this brokerage going to help me build and grow my business?"

The most important part of a brokerage is the training, and that includes training the agents' new recruits.

Because training is so vital to your success as a broker, you need to be able to boldly answer prospective agents, "Yes, we do have the best training around!" You will, when Sellstate is involved.

Sellstate Is the Only Company to Handle Back Office Administration Tasks on Your Behalf

As your brokerage beings to grow, a new challenge will arise. Handling the daily back office administration tasks begin to become overwhelming, and we have seen countless brokers lose their momentum and struggle because of it. In some extreme cases, we have had brokers tell us that they do not want to recruit any more agents because they already have too much to do, and every agent means another hour or two at the office doing administrative work.

The simple task of paying commissions becomes a burden as your office starts to close 30, 40, 50, or 100 transactions a month. Many companies will offer some form of back office accounting software intended to make your life easier, but that software is often very expensive and difficult to learn, which leads to expensive administrative training costs. In addition, your business now becomes tied to that one administrator. If that person ever leaves or misses work, you are left with a massive mess on your hands.

With Sellstate's exclusive C.P. Technology, all of the agent commissions are distributed electronically on your behalf. You never have to worry about writing a commission check. In addition, the C.P. Technology also electronically collects the fees that agents owe to the office for you. At the end of the year, C.P Technology distributes the 1099s, which alleviates that burdensome task from you as well.

Best of all, this requires no special software on your end. An administrator who is familiar with Microsoft Office can learn the process over the phone in a few minutes. It is that simple, which is why Sellstate's C.P. Technology is truly a game changer!

Sellstate Provides Technology

Technology is not optional in this business. In order to succeed you need to have it and use it. Sellstate believes so strongly in this that we provide the most comprehensive technology package to both brokers and your agents through Sellstate Power Suite.

You and your agents will have access to some of the most important tools, which include:

- A mobile responsive website that has IDX integration

- A CRM that automatically adds any leads you receive into it, saving you time and effort while making you more efficient
- A Comprehensive CMA and Buyer Tour creation tool
- Email drip campaigns that are customizable and ready to send
- A full neighborhood demographic report customizable to any area in the country
- A design center that allows for quick creation of marketing tools
- A full marketing center that allows for professional level pieces to be created and sent directly to an online printer
- Automatic promotion of your listings on the most prominent home search websites
- Lead generation through enhanced listings on Homes.com
- And much much more…

Sellstate Offers Great Tools

Agents and brokers need a lot of tools. Some agents may not even be aware of all their needs, but whether they are or not, the fact remains that agents have specific needs for quite a few tools.

Sellstate tools are unique, proven, and we are proud to say, better than you will find anywhere else. It is all included.

For example:

- Need to learn how to write a letter to send to people? (Included)
- Know what to send to a first-time home buyer versus a seasoned buyer? (Included)
- Know what to send to your sphere of influence? (Included)
- Need to know what to include in your office when you open? (Included)
- Need to know the size your office should be? (Included)
- Need to know the layout and design for your office? (Included)
- Need to know what IT and phone system to use? (Included)

Tools such as these usually come with a big price tag, but not at Sellstate. You will not believe what we charge brokers for our comprehensive list of tools that they get to use with their agents!

Sellstate Offers Savings on Supplies

It costs a lot to provide agents with what they need. Most brokers are not too keen to offer it all because it can be expensive.

When the reality of the costs per agent rise to the surface, we have heard brokers say, "I cannot afford to have 20 agents, much less 100!"

At Sellstate, we have economies of scale and design efficiency, which lowers the individual costs per agent considerably. And that means you can recruit more agents!

> The most important part of your brokerage is recruiting productive agents ... It is the lifeblood of your business.

With Sellstate, brokers know their agents have the right tools, and the brokers have the most efficient layout and setup, making the process very smooth.

Sellstate Shows You How

Agents have different needs. The new agents need one thing, the established 60% in the middle need another thing, and the top producers need something entirely different. Do you know how to meet those needs?

Sellstate knows exactly what your agents need at each level ... and provides that for your brokerage. Your agents have the know-how to get things done, and that translates right to your bottom line!

This is great peace of mind for you as well as for your agents. It is hard to put an accurate value on peace of mind.

Sellstate Has the Ultimate Package

No matter what your needs or where your business is, Sellstate has the tools, expertise, and patience to make sure you are equipped, trained, and confident to get yourself to the next level.

Your Next Step

Basically, everything you have read in this book ... that is what Sellstate provides to its brokers.

That means that your agents, the 30, 50, or 100 agents (or whatever number you aim for) you want to recruit to create your brokerage, will have direct access to everything you have read and learned.

The best trained team always wins, and that means you and your brokerage are getting a big push in the right direction ... toward your intended success.

To say it another way:

> When you become a broker with Sellstate, we go out of our way to help you become successful.

That's what we do.

If you are serious about wanting to build a brokerage with productive agents... call us.

Taking Decisive Action

It is always time to take action. The best action is the best-planned because it always brings the best results.

How I am going to think differently ...

_____

_____

_____

_____

_____

_____

_____

_____

_____

_____

_____

What I am going to do now (besides calling Sellstate to book an appointment):

_____

_____

_____

_____

_____

_____

_____

_____

_____

_____

Notes to self:

_____

_____

_____

_____

_____

_____

_____

_____

_____

_____

_____

_____

_____

_____

_____

_____

_____

_____

_____

_____

_____

_____

_____

_____

_____

_____

_____

_____

Conclusion

When preparation meets opportunity, amazing things happen! Some call it luck, but those of us in the real estate business, we know better.

At Sellstate, we are the preparation, support, and expertise part of the equation. You have the opportunity in your local area to open a brokerage. When we combine these two together ... the future is great!

This is about you, a real estate professional, and achieving your financial dreams.

We are here to help you do just that!

Once again, if you are serious about wanting to build a brokerage with productive agents... call us.

Notes to self:

_____

_____

_____

_____

_____

_____

_____

_____

_____

_____

_____

_____

_____

_____

_____

_____

_____

_____

_____

_____

_____

_____

_____

_____

_____

_____

_____

_____

Art Darmanin, Chief Executive Officer and Co-founder

Arthur Darmanin has more than 40 years of experience in the real estate industry, 29 of those years are combined managerial experience at the Broker and Regional Franchisor levels.

He has successfully managed several real estate offices before opening his own. Within three years, he expanded to owning four successful offices which controlled 51% market share. He then joined a 100% commission concept franchise and within two  years, purchased the regional franchise rights to a territory which he successfully developed.

This extraordinary success led to an executive position on the corporate team where he managed 80 franchises with over 3,000 salespeople in addition to maintaining his own regional territory.

Darmanin has experience in all facets of real estate including being a sales person, broker, instructor, former board president, franchisee, and franchisor. He is involved in all aspects of the business concentrating on the design and continuous evolution of the Sellstate system, franchising, brokers support, administration, marketing programs, and promotions.

Highlights:

- Over 40 years of experience in real estate
- Member of the executive team for one of the largest real estate companies in North America, managing thousands of agents and brokerages
- Built a successful region from the ground up
- Served as President of his association
- Managed his first real estate brokerage 2 years into his career
- As an independent broker, built the large brokerage in his market area with 6 offices in just 3 short years
- Member of O.R.E.A. Faculty of Education
- Co-founder and CEO of Sellstate

Neil Cresswell, President and Co-founder

Neil Cresswell has more than 25 years in the real estate industry. His career started in real estate in his early twenties, and he immediately rose to the top in sales for his entire area. Neil quickly became one of Canada's top real estate executives. Soon after, he became a broker/owner and eventually partnered in with Arthur Darmanin in the city's most successful office before taking control on his own.

By age 28, and having already surpassed the accomplishments of most in the industry, he purchased regional rights for the second largest real estate company in Canada in the nation's largest metropolitan city.

After enjoying all the success that he could in Canada, Neil moved to Florida and quickly became one of the leading Realtors in the United States. His continued success as a Realtor, broker, owner and regional owner lead him to co-create Sellstate with his longtime friend and business associate, Arthur Darmanin.

Neil is involved with every aspect of Sellstate and has a personal mission to help brokers and agents achieve their highest goals while developing a culture to exceed customer expectations. He spends a large amount of the year traveling the country to support and educate brokers and agents.

Highlights:

- Over 25 years of experience in real estate
- Carried an average inventory of 200+ non-REO listings
- Single-handedly outperformed entire brokerages
- National Trainer
- Immediately rose to the top in sales for his area and proceeded to become one of the top Realtors in the country
- Regional Franchisor of one of the largest Franchises in North America
- Co-founder and President of Sellstate

Michael Darmanin, Chief Operating Officer

Michael Darmanin is the Chief Operating Officer for Sellstate. He graduated with an Honours Baccalaureate in Commerce with Specialization in Marketing from the University of Ottawa, School of Management. Having attended one of the top four-year business schools in Canada with International accreditations, he is well versed in a wide array of business techniques and strategies.

Prior to his studies in management and marketing, Michael spent two years at the University of Ottawa studying in Computer and Electrical Engineering. The combination of marketing and engineering makes him the perfect candidate to lead Sellstate's technological innovations.

He joined Sellstate in 2006 and since then has spearheaded many of the marketing or technological advancements, including website design, brand image, Sellstate Power Suite creation, training programs, and cloud-based integration. He is central to the current social media strategy.

You may contact Michael through:

- Facebook.com/SellstateCOO
- Twitter: @SellstateCOO

Notes to self:

_____

_____

_____

_____

_____

_____

_____

_____

_____

_____

_____

_____

_____

_____

_____

_____

_____

_____

_____

_____

_____

_____

_____

_____

_____

_____

_____

_____

Notes to self:

_____

_____

_____

_____

_____

_____

_____

_____

_____

_____

_____

_____

_____

_____

_____

_____

_____

_____

_____

_____

_____

_____

_____

_____

_____

_____

_____

_____

Notes to self:

_____

_____

_____

_____

_____

_____

_____

_____

_____

_____

_____

_____

_____

_____

_____

_____

_____

_____

_____

_____

_____

_____

_____

_____

_____

_____

_____

_____

_____

_____

_____

www.Sellstate.com